# LILLII
# THE LEG

## The Life of Lillie Langtry

by

Tessa Coleman

'Mrs Langtry was ever an absorbing study. Possessing in a marked degree every feminine charm — wiles, fascination and moods — she was at the same time possessed of an iron will power, immense courage and a gift of instant decision which the captain of a 50,000 ton liner in a critical situation might envy. Remarkably well-read, it was with me always a surprise that she found time for her reading for I have never known any topic — and I use the word "any" deliberately — literature, science, arts or any other subject which she was unable to discuss with specialists. Hers was always a big and broad mind which could not tolerate anything commonplace or futile and her favourite phrase is indicative of her nature; "Don't let's fuss, please," spoken in a soft, plaintive voice, was a danger signal to those who knew her.'

*From 'Tramps of a Scamp' by Edward Michael.*

# SOCIÉTÉ JERSIAISE
# 1999

i

# LILLIE: THE LEGEND

## The Life of Lillie Langtry

Also by Tessa Coleman:

### Threads of History — The Jersey Occupation Tapestry

**Photographic acknowledgements and permissions**

**Front cover:** Lillie Langtry by Herbert Schmalz, Madame Tussaud's Archives, London.

**Back cover:** St. Saviour's church and Lillie's marble bust, Gareth Syvret.

**Other illustrations:** Sir Ian Malcolm, KCMG, Jeanne-Marie and Mary; Mary McFadean. Lillie Langtry by H. Weighall; Ian Appleton. King Edward VII's funeral procession, "PA" News, London. Tessa Coleman as Lillie with Mary Malcolm; Jersey Evening Post, Jersey. Oscar Wilde, Queen Victoria, portraits of Lillie; the Lafayette Collection. Sarah Bernhardt, Victoria and Albert Picture Library, London. Lillie, Millais' portrait, Miles' triptych, Frith's Academy, Louis Battenberg, travelling case, Roy Bean's saloon, Judge Roy Bean; Jersey Museums Service, Jersey. Lillie as a girl, St. Saviour's rectory, the Dean and family, Edward Langtry, the Prince of Wales, Arthur Jones, Lillie as Kate, Freddie Gebhardt, the White Ladye, Merman, Le Lys, Lady de Bathe, her coffin, her signature; Société Jersiaise, Jersey. St. Saviour's church, Gareth Syvret.

ISBN 0 9018907 24 8

# Contents

SOCIÉTÉ JERSIAISE

# Introduction

HAVING written a TV documentary, a radio drama series and a stage play on the subject of Lillie Langtry, I thought that she and I had gone as far as we could go together. But here I am writing a little book about her and last year the Jersey Heritage Trust asked me to portray the lady herself in the Kleinwort Benson Living History Exhibition at the Jersey Museum for their 'Lillie Langtry' season.

Four times a day, five days a week, I would spend 25 minutes or so playing the Jersey Lily and recalling her history for anyone who cared to listen. My audiences came in all shapes, sizes, ages and nationalities. Given the odd exception they had one thing in common — a fascination for Lillie Langtry. It was a salutary experience. What charisma did Jersey's most famous daughter hold over the public mind both in her day and ours?

She was, of course, extraordinarily famous — with a life packed with incident and more than a little scandal. In her youth she was renowned as the epitome of Pre-Raphaelite beauty and became the mistress of the future Edward VII. But there was so much more to her than that. She was a famous actress in her own right, a leader of society, a trail blazer in the art of woman's emancipation but, perhaps, most importantly of all, she was a muse and an inspiration to the likes of Oscar Wilde, John Everett Millais, James Whistler and Edward Poynter, to name but a few.

'Loveliness immortal', a poet once wrote of Lillie in life, and in death she remains so through the pen and paint portraits those worthies left behind. Mrs Langtry is ever-intriguing, fascinating and enigmatic. She was compliant and manipulative, audacious and demure, generous and acquisitive — a mass of incongruities. It is difficult to pin down Lillie's character and allure. What follows is my brief attempt to do so. I hope I have done her justice. She was an amazing woman.

*Tessa Coleman, Jersey, 1999*

'The Jersey Lily' — Tessa Coleman in period costume at the Jersey Museum
with Mary Malcolm, Lillie Langtry's grand-daughter

# Childhood and Marriage

IT is fun to picture Emilie Charlotte Le Breton (as Lillie Langtry was born) growing up in the idyllic surroundings of Victorian Jersey. A little island, set just off the coast of France with lush green valleys, long sandy beaches, horses and carriages and soft faced cows.

The pretty little girl, in Victorian ruffles and petticoats, was born into a reasonably affluent, male-dominated family. She would become the only girl amongst six brothers and as her father was The Dean of Jersey, (the head of Jersey's Anglican church), the family lived in St Saviour's Rectory, just a stone's throw from the parish church.

Lillie, as she soon came to be known, was born on October 13th, 1853. Across the water in England Victoria was Queen; a woman of thirty-five, and monarch of the greatest industrial nation of the world. She was already the mother of eight and her son and heir, Bertie, the Prince of Wales, with whom Lillie would later become rather intimately acquainted, was twelve years old and already a problem to his mother, being both wilful and disobedient.

In Jersey, Lillie led a carefree, happy childhood, growing up an incorrigible tomboy and joining in with her brothers' youthful pranks. She could swim, ride and sail at a very early age but she also had a keen and inquiring mind. Whilst her brothers all attended the local public school of Victoria College, Lillie was tutored at home. She was tri-lingual — French, English and Jèrrias ( the local French-Norman patois) all came naturally to her. The Dean also saw to it that her lessons included Latin, mathematics and history.

The Le Breton children were little devils. They would haunt the rectory graveyard at dead of night dressed in sheets to frighten the neighbours, steal door knockers and knock people's

**Lillie, when a young girl**

**St Saviour's rectory, Lillie's childhood home**

hats off with string tied across the driveway. Lillie remembered these happy pranks, the family's rose-strewn granite dwelling and their numerous pets with great affection all her life. Along with the picnics, band concerts and military reviews, these simple pleasures all made up her joyous early years.

As a youngster she could be seen galloping fearlessly across the sand dunes, her Titian brown hair streaming out behind her in the wind. At other times, though, we can picture her sitting quietly with a book, eager to learn about life. From her brothers she learnt a healthy competitive rivalry that stood her in good stead for the future.

This independent, strong willed child gave way to an accomplished, intelligent teenager with 'a certain something' right from the start. Not all of us today can see the great beauty that Lillie was reputed to possess. Her photographs are, of course, in black and white and that perhaps holds the key to our dilemma. They do not capture her creamy, flawless complexion and the dewy, violet eyes, nor her beautifully modulated voice. Whatever it was, her charms were very apparent to the opposite sex from an early age. Indeed she received her first marriage proposal at the tender age of fourteen.

Lieutenant Longley, a young army officer and son of the then Archbishop of Canterbury, was sent away with a flea in his ear by Lillie's reverend father when he asked for his daughter's hand. We can only guess what the emotional home-life must have been like between Dean Le Breton and his wife Emilie. He had met and married the pretty young woman in England before returning to his island birthplace. How long was it one wonders before his wife found out about the Dean's fatal flaw — for flaw there was.

We know a little about Lillie's discovery of her father's weakness as she was to tell the story quite late in life. It must have been a shock indeed for the young girl, who patently adored her handsome and liberal minded papa, to find him not to be the paragon of virtue she had always imagined.

It seems that, at the age of fourteen, Little took a fancy to a local boy she knew. Her father, seeing them walking innocently together one day, summoned her to his study and in uncompromising terms forbade her ever to see the boy again. It was so unlike her fond papa to be unfair that Lillie begged for a reason and couldn't understand why her father got so heated on the subject. Then, of course, he told her, and things were never the same between them again. The boy in question turned out to be her own half brother — her father's son by a local Jerseywoman. And that wasn't all. This revelation led to the knowledge that there were several other half siblings dotted about the island. Her father was not just the Dean of Jersey, but a libidinous philanderer as well.

**The Dean, Mrs Le Breton, Lillie and one of her brothers**

It is not too fanciful to surmise that this information coloured Lillie's attitude towards men from then on.

'Men were meant to be slaves,' she would say, years later, 'Can I help it if they subjugate themselves so easily?'

One can speculate that the disclosure about her father's failings prompted Lillie's ambition to leave the island.

The older she got, the more people remarked on her burgeoning beauty. One neighbour who particularly noticed this was Lord Suffield, who also had extensive property in London.

Thus, when Lillie was about sixteen, and on a short visit to London with her mother, the pair were invited to the Suffields' society ball. Although decked out in the most opulent finery Jersey had to offer, Lillie was appalled to feel so peasant-like next to the fine ladies of London society. She was actually mistaken for one of the maids! She didn't know how to dance the waltz nor which knife and fork to pick up at the dinner beforehand. Shamed by her lack of social graces and country apparel, she was, none the less, captivated by the excitement, colour and glamour of this privileged life and resolved to enter it herself one day. She would return, she vowed, and take London by storm.

Back in Jersey she set about bettering herself; learning how to dance the latest dances, how to dress and converse properly — whilst all the while looking for her way of escape. She adored her island birthplace but her father's liaisons made it imperative for her to get away. She realised that the only way to achieve the lifestyle she craved, of money and position, was to marry it. She had many admirers but none seemed quite right for her purposes.

Then, one day, a fine yacht came into the harbour at St Aubin's Bay and, as she remarked carelessly years later: 'To be mistress of the yacht I married the owner'. The man she set about captivating was Edward Langtry, a wealthy young Irish widower and friend of her brother, William. Lillie was impressed not only by Edward's yacht, 'The Red Gauntlet', and the other two he owned, but also by his generosity in providing a sumptuous wedding party for her brother at the Island's yacht club. This appeared to her to be just the sort of lifestyle she was looking for. Perhaps she convinced herself she was in love with him. Who can say? It seems unlikely. Edward was an introverted, morose young man, still smarting from the death of his first wife.

His family were ship owners in Belfast and Edward was a man of independent means, living mostly off rents from properties in Ireland. He was also somewhat of an idler with no interest in a profession, and best content when either sailing or, preferably, fishing. Edward was easily captured. Lillie's family, however, were not. Her parents thought her too young to marry and wanted her to have at least one season in London. Her brothers, especially the youngest, Reggie, were vehemently against the union. Indeed, a blazing row about her forthcoming nuptials resulted in a very painful estrangement from her youngest sibling.

**Edward Langtry**

As ever, though, when Lillie had made up her mind about something, she always got her way. And so, at the age of just twenty, on March 9th, 1874, she married Edward Langtry at St. Saviour's church, with her father officiating, despite his misgivings. Only one brother was present at the low-key affair and Edward and Lillie sailed away on their honeymoon in 'The Red Gauntlet' with few to rejoice at their union.

# London and Fame

BOTH Edward and Lillie were disappointed in their marriage. Lillie, with her determination and ambition, was no substitute for Edward's first compliant and uncomplaining wife. Lillie had wanted to settle straight away in London, but this was too expensive for Edward's pocket, which soon proved not as deep as his new wife had fondly imagined. Lillie consoled herself that her first home, although in Jersey, was the prestigious Noirmont Manor in the lovely surroundings of Belcroute Bay, St Brelade.

She was, however, anxious for pastures new, and persuaded Edward to move to England. Before leaving she left her signature cut into a windowpane at Noirmont, as she had done at the rectory before. It is perhaps significant that Lillie's self-confidence was such that she thought it worthwhile to leave her mark in this manner at such an early stage of her life.

The Langtrys' first house in England was in Southampton and, although an impressive residence, the provinces were not where Lillie's ambitions lay. Then she became dangerously ill with typhoid fever and very nearly died. The doctor who attended her advised a change of air for her convalescence and, incredibly, allowed her to persuade him and her husband that London, that insanitary, smoky metropolis would be the perfect spot. It had taken a while but, as usual, Lillie got what she wanted.

Edward's fortune was already dwindling. Yachts had to be sold to cover Lillie's doctor's expenses and the move to the capital. Her arrival in London was not as auspicious as she might have hoped, but at least she was there — if only in rented accommodation at Eaton Place. Lillie's cold fish of a husband now became one completely out of water.

He mourned the loss of his country pursuits and became

increasingly frustrated in trailing around after his wife to theatres, galleries and museums. Quite simply, they were bored with each other, and whilst Lillie began taking to her bed with a good book, Edward was drawn more and more to the bottle. Then news came from Jersey that stung them out of their lethargy.

Lillie's brother, Reggie, the one she had been closest to but had quarrelled with so bitterly over her marriage, had died after a fall from his horse. She was devastated and made a heartbreaking journey back to Jersey to try and comfort her mother who had already lost two sons who had died abroad in the service of the Queen. Returning to London after Reggie's funeral, Lillie took with her an Italian maid, Dominique, who would remain a faithful companion and servant for many years.

Edward and Lillie continued their listless London life once again until a chance encounter changed their lives forever. A meeting with another former Jersey neighbour, Lord Ranelagh, led to an invitation to society hostess Lady Sebright's soirée . Henceforth life for the Langtry's would never be the same again. Lillie would later recount that she and her husband were so poor by that time that she had but two dresses to her name. As it happened, she remained in mourning for Reggie and went to the fashionable soirée in a plain black dress, her hair knotted artlessly at the nape of her neck and devoid of any jewellery, because she had none.

Many of London's famous artists and politicians gathered at the Sebrights' Monday evening affairs. The likes of John Millais, Henry Irving and James Whistler were just some of those who witnessed and marvelled as the Langtrys made an unobtrusive entrance into their midst and all eyes turned onto the stunning young woman in black. Many of those assembled were aesthetes — they appreciated beauty and were eager to

The simple, unadorned Lillie with her hair in the 'Langtry knot'

celebrate it. The plainly dressed, unadorned Lillie found herself surrounded by male admirers clamouring for her attention whilst poor Edward was totally ignored and left to fade into the background — a state of affairs that was to continue for as long as the marriage lasted. Her 'cavaliers', as she called them, all begged to be allowed to take her in to supper but her countryman, John Everett Millais, won the day.

He was a giant amongst contemporary painters and a leader of the pre-Raphaelite movement. By the end of the party he had elicited a promise from Lillie to sit for him and his portrait of 'A Jersey Lily' was to make her immortal.

That party was the start of Lillie's rapid rise to fame. The next day she and her husband were inundated with invitations to many of the finest balls and parties in the heart of London society. To take London by storm had been her ambition. It had taken her a year, but she had now done it! Whilst Edward remained unenthusiastic, Lillie revelled in it. She soon became what was known in those days as a 'P.B.'. This stood for 'Professional Beauty' who were the decorative creatures in Society whom the masses tried to copy. And they certainly tried to copy Lillie Langtry!

Her portrait was now sold by the hundreds on postcards at a penny a time. Magazines and newspapers showed off the 'Langtry Hat', the 'Langtry Shoes' and the famous ''Langtry Knot', the simple hairstyle she had so innocently created. Her fame grew and grew. She began to be mobbed wherever she went and people gathered outside her little house just to catch a glimpse of her. It was all very gratifying.

Then there were the paintings. Lillie's own personal favourite was 'A Jersey Lily'. Millais had said that she was the most exasperating subject he had ever attempted: 'You look just beautiful for fifty-five minutes of an hour, but for the other five, you are amazing,' he told her.

16

**John Everett Millais' 'A Jersey Lily'**

The Miles' triptych

He wanted to paint her as he had first set eyes on her in the by now famous black dress and unadorned hair. His portrait presents a shy, demure young woman, predominantly in hues of black and grey.

The artist then decided that it needed a splash of colour for greater impact and remembered the Jersey lily from Lillie's island home. Lillie duly sent away for the flower and was upset to discover that the one her mother so carefully forwarded to her was, in fact, of the Guernsey variety!

It was added to the portrait and entitled 'A Jersey Lily'— neverthless. By the time the portrait was first displayed in 1879, Lillie's celebrity was such that it had to be roped off behind velvet cords to keep it from harm, so many people wanted to see it.

'A Jersey Lily' was named picture of the year on three different occasions. Other artists who queued up to paint her included Edward Burne-Jones, James Whistler and Edward Poynter. The latter saw Lillie quite differently to Millais. This is no virginal girl but a sensual woman in a low-necked yellow silk gown. Lillie never liked it, saying she felt he hadn't captured her colouring. Once it had been displayed at the Burlington

**Portrait of Mrs Langtry by Edward Poynter**

gallery, however, the artist made her a present of it. She in turn lent it to a new and rather special friend, who kept it on a sort of altar in celebration of her beauty.

A lesser artist was actually the first to capture Lillie Langtry's likeness. Frank Miles had been present at the Sebrights' party. 'Who is she?' he said, as she first appeared— ''the Greek goddess in the black dress?' As Lillie was being surrounded by admirers, the young man had buzzed around her like an irksome fly, capturing her image on the back of an envelope. Although he then presented it to her 'along with my heart', he quickly made another sketch to be mass-produced on postcards. One of Frank's sketches of Lillie gave her her first brush with Royalty.

Prince Leopold, Queen Victoria's youngest son, bought it and hung it in his room at Buckingham Palace. The Queen, discovering a 'P.B.' residing in her son's bedroom, climbed onto a chair and removed the offending picture with her own hands, having it disposed of by a footman. Right from the start, as far as Mrs Langtry was concerned, Victoria was not amused!

It was also through Frank Miles that Lillie first met Oscar Wilde — the young men shared a house together. Oscar was only twenty two and recently graduated from Oxford University. He became her friend, adviser and champion, describing her as 'simply the most beautiful woman in the world' and even more sumptuously as 'Lillie Langtry, arising like Venus from the Jersey foam'.

It was he who displayed Poynter's portrait of Lillie in a little shrine in his front room. Truth to tell, Oscar was as desperate for fame and fortune as his new friend was, and he rather hitched a ride on Lillie's shooting star.

He wrote a poem to her loveliness (or in fact simply adapted one he had already written) dedicating it 'to the new Helen, formerly of Troy, now of London'.

**Oscar Wilde', from his 'carte de visite', late 1880s**

For a while he seemed to be quite obsessed by her. He would sleep all night on her doorstep, so that the bewildered Edward Langtry would trip over him in the early hours on his unsteady way into the house.

Oscar would carry a single lily to Lillie's front door every day in tribute and was known on occasion to serenade her from the pavement outside her bedroom window. All of these extravagant

**Queen Victoria**

gestures seem carefully calculated to enhance the pair's celebrity. Oscar, it appears, was busy creating a legend. He had become, as he put it, 'an apostle of the lily'.

Lillie even became one of the first famous faces to endorse a commercial product. It was for Pears Soap. She simply lent her photograph and signature beneath an endorsement saying that she used and liked the product. For that she was paid £132. There was a reason for the odd amount of money — no one seemed to know what a suitable fee would be, so Lillie merely charged her weight in pound notes! As Lillie became increasingly talked about and celebrated there was one member of society who was particularly keen to meet 'the new phenomenon' — Bertie, the Prince of Wales himself.

**Lillie Langtry by H. Weighall**

# Bertie, The Prince of Wales

WHEN Lillie first met the Prince of Wales, in 1877, he was a man of thirty-five, bearded and bewhiskered and a debonair, rather rakish playboy about town. He was a married man (his wife, the beautiful Princess Alexandra turned a blind eye to his indiscretions), and the father of five. His disapproving mother kept him from high office so that Bertie, or Albert Edward as he was christened, had become simply a 'prince of pleasure'. The leader of the fashionable and aristocratic Marlborough House Set, he lived a life full of trips abroad, country house parties, concerts, theatres, yachting, dining, dancing and seducing. Yes, Bertie collected pretty woman like other men might have collected stamps.

It's tempting to think that Bertie might have first seen Mrs Langtry on the wall of his brother's bedroom before their mother removed her picture. At any event he had certainly heard all about her, through the inevitable society grapevine, and was more than anxious to make her acquaintance. Bertie's good friend, Sir Alan Young, was pressed into service. He gave a small and select dinner party at his home to which the Langtrys were invited. Lillie would have us believe in her autobiography that she knew nothing of the Prince's presence, and as he was late, his sudden appearance was a shock to both her husband and herself. For a moment she explains, whilst Edward choked into his inevitable glass at the sight of him, Lillie thought of climbing up the chimney to distance herself from this august personage. I take this with a pinch of salt. I think Lillie must have been delighted at the Prince's appearance and, due to his obvious interest in her, more than a little aware that she was the reason for it. She was placed next to him at dinner and we can imagine the coy, lowered glances of the young woman as His Royal Highness eyed up his next possible conquest.

**The Prince of Wales at 35**

Lillie and Bertie obviously liked what they saw on that first meeting for they soon became lovers. What Edward felt about being cuckolded so obviously we can only imagine for he has left no comments on the subject.

Bertie, as his own wife Alexandra described him, was 'a very naughty little man'. There had been many mistresses of all shapes, sizes and class — he was nothing if not eclectic in his taste. But, with Lillie, the relationship would be different. Whilst with previous relationships Bertie had at least made a pretence of discretion (even if it hadn't always worked), with Lillie he positively flaunted the affair. She became his first publicly acknowledged mistress. Hostesses knew that if Mrs Langtry was not invited to a ball or house party, then Bertie would probably not turn up either. They became very much a couple, even travelling abroad together, whilst still married to their respective spouses.

What Lillie saw in Bertie is easy to imagine. Power, wealth and position are powerful aphrodisiacs. But she also liked and admired him. He was affable, spoilt, kindly and volatile. Plus, she reflected, she always felt slightly frightened of him, which intrigued her.

And what of Bertie? Lillie amused and diverted him. Apart from the obvious charms of the lovely twenty-four-year-old Jerseywoman, he was attracted to her independence of spirit and the fact that she refused to be subservient. Especially, there was their shared, somewhat childish sense of humour. They would join in silly practical jokes against their long suffering friends — making them apple pie beds, racing down staircases on silver trays, even hoisting a donkey into a friend's bedroom, where the long suffering guest found it on his bed complete with mob-cap! Another shared delight were the pet dogs they surrounded themselves with all their lives. Bertie would keep Lillie supplied from his kennels in Sandringham.

The definitive 'P.B.'

The impoverished Langtrys found themselves suddenly in funds, probably partly because of all the credit allowed to the by now famous couple. They moved to a bigger house where Lillie could entertain more easily. Her black dress (which she had worn day and night, simply turning down the collar to make it more decolleté for the evening), literally fell apart and it was replaced by increasingly opulent gowns and negligeés of the finest silks and satins.

Where before Bertie had given trinkets and gems to his conquests, Lillie received a house. Built from scratch in Bournemouth, she named it 'The Red House' and stamped it with her own special mark and humour from top to bottom.

Completed in 1877, the foundation stone bore the date and Lillie's initials E.L.L. — Emilie Le Breton Langtry. The same initials would adorn the oak mantlepiece inside. The motto of her house was delightfully ambiguous — 'They say — what say they? Let them say'. Another motto in the hall greeted guests: 'And yours, too, my friend'.

The Red House was very much in two sections. On one side of the house were Lillie's fairly modest but feminine rooms and, on the other side, a much grander set of suites for Bertie. From the Prince's room Lillie thoughtfully had a little hatch made into the wall so he could keep an eye on who arrived on the other side. Here the lovers could relax in comfort and quiet when they were both able to slip away from their unsatisfying marriages.

The trysts were possible because Edward Langtry went away on fishing trips more and more, travelled abroad or merely indulged in home-bound drinking binges. Alexandra, too, often travelled without her husband. But truth to tell, she knew all about his new lady love. In some ways it seemed she almost approved and never showed anything but genuine concern and friendship for Lillie.

The adorned and fashionable Lillie

Perhaps as a reward for the happiness she had brought him, Bertie decided that Lillie should have the respectability that being presented at court would bring. By this time the Queen's beloved Albert had died of typhoid fever and Queen Victoria held her presentations with the help of Bertie and Alix. Although the 'drawing rooms' were primarily for eighteen-year-old debutantes, some older women were also presented and thus accepted into society's upper echelons.

One can imagine that Lillie felt a certain amount of trepidation at coming face to face with Bertie's imperious little mother. The Queen, like the rest of the court, knew all about Mrs Langtry's liaison with her son. Would she snub Lillie? Perhaps refuse to take her hand when presented? It was not beyond the bounds of possibility that Lillie might become the centre of a very public humiliation. But Bertie insisted that: 'it should be done', his word was law and, after all, Lillie never lacked courage.

Bertie paved the way for Lillie by first having Edward presented some time before. Victoria was sufficiently curious about the cuckolded husband to spend a full five minutes with the unfortunate man. Lillie did not fare so well.

She eventually made her curtsey at a May drawing room in 1878. Her mother had travelled from Jersey to rehearse her for the great event. Lillie wore an ivory brocade gown and a nine foot court train that hung from the shoulders. Bertie had thoughtfully sent her a bouquet of Marachel roses that complimented her outfit perfectly. Lillie practised curtsying until her knees ached.

She rehearsed how to catch her train that the pages would gather up and throw to her and how to make a dignified backwards exit. However, Lillie's sense of fun couldn't resist a little joke even on this solemn occasion. In her hair she placed three long ostrich plumes, which everyone said called to mind The

Prince of Wales coat of arms. The accompanying motto for the fleur de lys was: 'I serve'.

By arriving late for the beginning of the presentation Lillie had gambled that the Queen, as she often did, would have retired and let Alix take over. But Victoria was sufficiently curious to meet her son's mistress to stay for the duration and was not best pleased that Lillie was second to last.

When the momentous meeting finally occurred it was rather a let-down.

The Queen barely seemed to acknowledge Lillie, staring straight in front of her, extending her hand in a perfunctory manner without a flicker of a smile. Lillie, having acquitted herself with panache, retired reflecting that it was all 'a great deal of labour lost'.

She was, though, duly presented and now socially acceptable to the highest in the land. An admirer had presented Lillie with a splendid horse, 'Redskin', and she rode in Rotten Row in a daily ritual with The Prince of Wales, a posse of adoring young men known as 'Langtry's Lancers' following in her wake; she attended the balls and parties of the Marlborough House set and could now appear at Buckingham Palace itself. She had come a long way from the little girl in ribbons and petticoats running wild in Jersey and she was proud of the journey.

Pride, however, as we know, comes before a fall.

A private view at the Royal

cademy, 1881, by W. P. Frith

# Prince Louis Battenberg

THOSE three years in the height of London society, mobbed, fêted and adored by the masses, indulged and kowtowed to by the aristocracy, were 'a dream, a delight, a wild excitement' for Lillie Langtry.

However, there was another side to her life. Not everyone approved of her lifestyle, and the editor of a magazine called Town Talk criticised her, hinted at a relationship with Bertie and reported that she and Edward were on the verge of divorce. Edward went to court to sue the man — Rossenberg — for libel. Rossenberg was summarily dispatched to jail, even though, essentially, he only spoke the truth.

Not so easily disposed of was the problem of the Langtrys violent overspending. The 'fairyland', as Lillie called the world she was living in, cost an inordinate amount of money to inhabit. Clothes, furnishings and the trappings of wealth like a horse and brougham all took money that the wretched Edward did not have.

So, too, Lillie's relationship with Bertie was undergoing a sea change. For three years she had been his first publicly acknowledged mistress and he was uncommonly faithful to her. But now, nearing his fortieth birthday, the blue eyes were beginning to roam again. Sarah Bernhardt was one of the women they alighted on and Lillie was disquieted enough by his attentions to the famous French actress to make a tremendous social gaffe. Although she would deny the story herself, according to friends the misdemeanour was true. She was overly familiar with the Prince at a fancy dress party he was attending with his wife, Princess Alexandra. In fact she went so far as to forget herself and tease him in public by putting ice down the back of his costume. It was Bertie now who was not amused, his dignity was damaged and Alix compromised.

**Prince Louis Battenberg**

He stormed out of the party and Lillie was out of favour not just with her royal lover but also with his sycophantic friends.

Whilst Lillie's fall from grace left Bertie free to dally elsewhere, Edward's slide towards alcoholism became more inexorable and Lillie's confidence needed bolstering.

Perhaps that is why she turned to one of her legion of admirers for consolation. As the Langtrys teetered on the brink of bankruptcy, with Bertie tasting pastures new and society in general cooling towards her, Lillie found the time opportune to fall in love. The gentleman in question was Prince Louis Battenberg, a German Prince from Hesse, Bertie's cousin and an officer in the British navy. A handsome, bearded fellow of twenty-six, he was a favourite with the ladies as well as Bertie whom he called 'Uncle'.

He had first met Lillie when she accompanied Bertie aboard the royal yacht Osborne on which he was a serving officer. Their relationship now progressed into something more intimate. At almost the same time as Edward was finally made bankrupt, Lillie discovered that she was pregnant with Louis' child.

When she had first left Jersey, Lillie had left behind a dear friend, called Arthur Jones. He was a young gentleman farmer, Lord Ranelagh's natural son and one of Lillie's earliest loves. She had kept up a passionate correspondence with 'Artie' over the years and had seen him whenever he was in London or she in Jersey.

She wrote to Arthur Jones for advice and solace and he became one of the few people privy to the secret that she was to have a child not by her husband. As Artie was reportedly in love with her himself, the news cannot have been particularly welcome to him.

With the bailiffs at the door (Dominique took to secreting trinkets in callers' pockets) and her effects sold at auction to

**Sarah Bernhardt as Hamlet**

**Arthur Jones**

pay off the creditors, Lillie fled to Jersey. She had no home there now, though.

Both her mother and the Jersey authorities had finally had enough of the Dean's philandering. He had been asked to leave the island and demoted to vicar in a slum of Marylebone. Lillie subsequently installed her mother at The Red House in Bournemouth.

Before Lillie left for Jersey, Bertie had showed his true colours to a friend in crisis. Their affair might, for the time being at least, be curtailed but now friendship took over. He counselled her that the Royal Family would never countenance her marrying Louis, even if she could get Edward to give her a divorce, which he doubted. Louis was sent away to sea in the unfortunately named battleship 'The Inconstant', and once it became obvious that she couldn't hide her condition in Jersey, Lillie went to France.

The plan was devised by the Prince of Wales himself.

Bertie, I'm sure, wanted to help his newly discarded mistress, but he was also inordinately fond of the young Louis Battenberg and wanted to keep his name as free from scandal as possible. He even had Edward Langtry sent away to America, ostensibly on princely business.

Edward was to know nothing of his wife's pregnancy nor the resulting child for many years to come.

Lillie was escorted to France by two of Bertie's emissaries. Once in Paris she was kept almost under guard, hardly allowed out, especially towards the end of her pregnancy.

She felt very alone and friendless. Irrevocably separated from her two recent royal lovers, she took to writing to a third — Arthur Jones — begging him to come to her.

As always, she got her way. Arthur Jones was one of the first people to see Lillie's child. Jeanne Marie was born in Paris in March, 1881.

# The Stage and America

WITH Jeanne Marie's birth, Lillie decided that her marriage to Edward Langtry was over. He knew nothing of the child but she had written to him asking for a divorce. Although Edward would always refuse to make it legal, the couple were ostensibly separated from then on and seldom, if ever, saw each other. Eventually, when an official separation was drawn up, Lillie would make Edward a monthly allowance through her lawyers but of his lifestyle she knew very little. The wretched man actually made a rapid decline into hopeless alcoholism.

Returning to London a bankrupt, Lillie somehow managed to rent accommodation in Ely Place. She secreted Jeanne Marie away in Bournemouth at The Red House with her mother and few knew that she had recently given birth.

If anyone ever came across the child, Lillie told them that she was the daughter of her brother Maurice, who had died abroad and whom she would be bringing up as her own. For the first ten years of her life little Jeanne Marie, who was brought up with French as her first language, thought of and referred to Lillie as *'ma tante'*. Even when she was told that Lillie was her mother, the lies didn't stop. Her father, she then gathered, was the absent Edward Langtry, whom she never saw.

Back in London, at Ely Place, Lillie realised for the first time in her life that she was going to have to make her own living. Her friends gave her helpful advice. Everything from opening a hat shop to becoming a market gardener were suggested. It was indirectly, however, through her friend, Oscar Wilde, that her thoughts settled firmly on the stage.

Lillie had thought about the theatre for some time — especially after becoming an avid fan of her rival, Sarah Bernhardt.

An acquaintance of Oscar's, Henrietta La Bouchère, a former actress, had heard of Lillie's interest and saw the opportunity

**Lillie as Kate Hardcastle**

to make some money. She arrived at Lillie's rooms and practically took her over. She coached the lovely Mrs Langtry for an amateur theatrical performance at Twickenham Town Hall. By Lillie's own account it was not a success. She forgot her lines and hated the experience, vowing never to set foot on a stage ever again. But Henrietta was made of stronger stuff. She had seen the interest generated by an appearance of the Prince of Wales' mistress and soon got Lillie involved in a charity Matinée at Squire Bancroft's Haymarket Theatre. The play was Goldsmith's ''She Stoops to Conquer', and Lillie was to play Kate Hardcastle. Lillie was the only amateur on stage.

Bertie and Alix were sitting in the Royal Box and the theatre was sold out, such was the interest in the infamous Mrs Langtry. Lillie was understandably nervous but, as she walked out on stage, there was a standing ovation for her and several others throughout the performance. This was not perhaps anything to do with her acting ability but more to do with her notoriety. The packed house and overflowing box office persuaded Squire Bancroft, like Henrietta before him, that there was a lot of money in Lillie Langtry and he signed her then and there for his professional company.

Lillie's career as an actress never looked back. Just a year later she found herself in America, with her own company, touring the length and breadth of the country and just as fêted and adored in that country as she was in her own. For a while Henrietta was her manager and made the first trip to America with her. Lillie's fame had preceded her. There to greet her on her arrival in New York harbour was a band playing 'God Save the Queen' and a tug full of photographers and reporters. In their midst, standing head and shoulders above the crowd, was an extraordinary looking man in a brown cap and green coat waving an enormous bunch of lilies in greeting. He was none other than Oscar Wilde, who was making his first lecture tour

**Lillie Langtry's travelling case**

of America. When the two Britons were reunited and surrounded by the press, Oscar pronounced that he would rather have discovered Mrs Langtry than to have discovered America. Later he explained that he intended to show her lots of different places and take lots of photographs — one of Niagara Falls as 'an unpretentious back drop'. It all made excellent copy and got both their names into the newspapers.

Ten years later, Oscar would actually write 'Lady Windermere's Fan' specifically for Lillie. She refused to play the part of a woman with a grown up illegitimate daughter, saying she was 'too young'. As she was nearing forty at the time, I can't help thinking that the plot might have been a little too close to home for Lillie. She must have regretted missing out on such a tremendous success.

The plays that Lillie performed in during her trips to America were contemporary dramas and Shakespeare. Reviews might

**Freddie Gebhardt**

have been mixed but box office receipts were extremely gratifying. The Prince of Wales' mistress drew enormous crowds
wherever she went, stopped traffic on Fifth Avenue, and the
strains of ''The Jersey Lily Waltz' were heard everywhere. On
that first trip, however, Henrietta didn't stay the course and
returned to England in a fit of pique, some of it to do with
Oscar monopolising Lillie's time plus, of course, the usual
army of admirers. Lillie now managed her own company with
aplomb, her maxim being, as it was all throughout her life, 'let
us not fuss, please,' said in such tones as to quell even the most
rebellious spirit.

Of prime importance, as far as admirers were concerned in
the Land of the Free, was a twenty-two-year-old, handsome
Baltimore millionaire, Freddie Gebhardt, who was a generous
lover — to say the least. Freddie was to shower Lillie with presents of every kind — the magnificent travelling case displayed at the Jersey Museum is believed to be one of them.
Freddie stayed in Lillie's life for several years, begging her to
marry him. She couldn't, because Edward Langtry refused to
allow her a divorce. So Freddie came up with the idea of Lillie
becoming an American citizen and obtaining an American
divorce. This was duly done in 1887, on the grounds that
Edward (who knew nothing about it) had deserted her!
However, despite this American divorce, Lillie continued in
her refusals to marry Freddie.

Freddie travelled everywhere with Lillie in America — she
spent five consecutive years touring there and then made many
other visits later. She used to call him her 'bodyguard', which
fooled few people but the scandal of their unwedded relationship did wonders for the box office, even though she was once
denounced in the American House of Representatives as
'degrading American Morals'. It was Freddie who was thought
to be responsible for the fine town house Lillie purchased in

Judge Roy Bean's homage to Lillie in Langtry, Texas

New York and also for the Thomas Mann railway carriage that transported her in the height of luxury from one American coast to the other. Lillie christened her perambulating palace 'The Lalee', meaning 'flirt'. It was an impressive sight and recognisable wherever she went. Costing in those days a quarter of a million dollars, she had it painted her favourite royal blue with a slash of golden lilies adorning the sides. Inside were ten rooms, including her own boudoir and salon, bathroom, kitchen and assorted guest rooms. She even had a piano on board plus a menagerie of pets. Occasionally Jeanne Marie would join her mother on board this splendid moving home.

It was in ''The Lalee' that Lillie finally visited the Little Texas town of Langtry. Previously run by the Wild West notoriety, Judge Roy Bean, the town was originally called Vinagaroon. However, Roy Bean had seen Lillie perform on stage in Chicago and developed an obsession for her. He wrote to her advising that he was renaming his town Langtry in her honour, that the saloon which doubled as his courthouse, was to be called The Jersey Lily and that her photograph adorned it everywhere. Lillie was not able to visit until after the judge, the self-styled 'Law West of the Pecos', had died. (He died peacefully in bed, incidentally, not in a shoot-out as Hollywood would have it). When Lillie finally got there, in 1894, the townspeople made a big fuss of her, presented her with the judge's pet bear which, thankfully, escaped, but also his gun which apparently 'kept law and order in the 'Jersey Lilly' Saloon *(sic)*.

Judge Roy Bean

Langtry, Texas, has changed little over the years; the saloon is still there — preserved as a museum to the charms of the Jersey Lily.

During her second season in America, Lillie had decided to sink a sizeable amount of the tremendous wealth she had accumulated into a ranch in California. It boasted six thousand acres and here she would ride to her heart's content, dressed in cowboy style. She had a string of racehorses stabled there and also set about cultivating and selling her own wine. After some years, though, several of her horses were killed in a railway accident and, disheartened with the project, she sold up.

It was during one of her American tours in 1888 that Lillie had news of her disgraced father, William le Breton. Although still on the books as The Dean of Jersey, he had died alone in Kennington, London, with a mere £5 to his name.

# The Races and Mr. Jersey

BACK in England, the monthly allowance to Edward continued, on the condition that he didn't 'pester' her. Consequently Lillie knew little, if anything, about his life in seedy lodgings consuming copious amounts of alcohol.

Louis Battenberg had married his cousin Victoria of Hesse and started a family. Freddie remained in Lillie's life but there were other suitors as well, two of whom took to fighting over her in the street! The Jersey Lily remained as notorious and as well publicised as ever.

Lillie had always been interested in horse racing, ever since her days of training up a young filly to run in the Jersey races. She had often attended Ascot and the like with Bertie and many of her friends were of the racing fraternity. For a while she had her own racing stables just outside Newmarket. But the man who got her seriously interested in the turf was a young and somewhat dissolute Scotsman called George Baird. Possessor of a large fortune and an unsavoury reputation, George, or Squire Abingdon as he termed himself, was a successful amateur jockey and womaniser. He had an unpleasant habit of roughing up his lady friends when in his cups and Lillie Langtry was to prove no exception. When a friend of hers asked why she stayed with the brute, Lillie replied that although she loathed him, every time he hit her he gave her five thousand pounds in recompense.

Once, however, George nearly went too far. Breaking in on a tryst between Lillie and a beau of hers in Paris, George destroyed the hotel room he found them in, beat her companion unconscious and put Lillie in hospital. She was going to press charges but, once more, George's wealth got him out of trouble. This time as recompense George offered her the beautiful White Ladye — a 220 foot racing yacht. Lillie's acquisi-

**The White Ladye**

tive nature got the better of her and, accepting the yacht, she dropped the charges. The American press, getting wind of this story, had a lot of fun in print, nicknaming the White Ladye 'The Black Eye'.

Lillie's first really successful horse, 'Milford' was also a present from George, and once Mrs Langtry got the bit between her teeth so to speak, there was no stopping her. She became a race horse owner in earnest, enjoying a friendly rivalry with her erstwhile lover and full-time friend The Prince of Wales. She raced under the name of 'Mr. Jersey' and became the first woman ever to set foot across the hallowed portals of the all male Jockey Club — on the arm of HRH, of course. Perhaps it was as well for Lillie's state of health that George Baird died soon afterwards, a victim of his dissipated lifestyle.

Lillie's most successful horse was 'Merman', which was to win her The Cesarewitch Cup in 1897, bringing in the princely amount of £120,000 at the time.

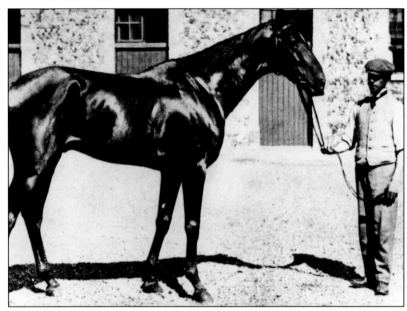
**Merman, winner of the 1897 Caesarewitch Cup**

Two days after this win, Lillie was informed that her husband, Edward Langtry, had died. Although she never saw him, she had continued his allowance which he spent mostly on drink. His alcoholism had led to his committal to a mental asylum in Chester, where he died with just a few pence in his pocket. The man who had dined with princes had come to a sad end indeed.

Edward's pitiful death left his widow completely free at last to marry again. There were many suitors around, although Freddie Gebhardt and Artie Jones had given up asking and married elsewhere. Three years after Edward's death, when she was forty five, Lillie finally consented to marry Hugo de Bathe. Nobody quite knew why.

He was an affable young aristocrat. Nineteen years younger than his bride, he was, perhaps, a more suitable suitor for Jeanne Marie. He was tall and reasonably handsome, but no intellectual and without a profession — similar, indeed, to

Lillie's first husband. He had a private income from his father Sir Henry, but the latter was so incensed by his son's unsuitable marriage that he cut them off without a penny. Lillie, as usual, was left to provide.

The couple married in secret in Jersey at St Saviour's Church on July 27th, 1899, on the same day that Merman made a splendid win at Goodwood. The new home Lillie had bought them in Jersey — a little cottage on the seashore at Beaumont, St Brelade was, naturally, called Merman — a name it retains in its altered state to this day. The couple also retained their houses in England.

When Hugo went off to fight in the Boer War Lillie, who had abandoned the stage for a while in favour of racing and who had amassed a considerable fortune from these two pursuits, returned to the theatre. Her public were delighted to see her back, none more so than her countrymen in Jersey.

In July 1900, Lillie took her controversial new play 'The Degenerates' (based heavily upon her own life) to the island to open Jersey's new theatre, The Opera House.

There were two schools of thought in Jersey on the subject of Lillie Langtry. One was that of local heroine and the other, that of a brazen hussy. It was the former group who attended the prestigious opening and gave her a warm and rousing reception, especially after her curtain speech which ended diplomatically with a recitation in Jersey French, the local patois: a recital which nearly brought the house down. Lillie certainly knew how to get an audience on her side.

In the year of Queen Victoria's death, 1901, when Bertie became king at the age of fifty nine, Lillie added theatre owner to her CV. She bought the enormous Imperial Theatre in London and spent a small fortune on refurbishing it. Although it was now a King and Queen who attended her first nights in the Royal Box, the theatre was difficult to fill, the project

St Saviour's Church, where Lillie Langtry married both her husbands, and where, eventually, the Lady de Bathe was buried

failed and the Imperial sold at a loss. Not everything Lillie touched turned to gold.

For Bertie's coronation, Lillie and a few of his other 'lady friends' from over the years were all invited to attend the ceremony at Westminster Abbey. Rather amusingly, they were all placed in the same pew together. What they thought of this state of affairs we will never know; but legend has it that the pew in question was irreverently nicknamed — 'The King's Loose Box'!

# The Later Years

THE story of Lillie's daughter Jeanne Marie ( or Jeanne as the girl soon liked to be called) is not a particularly happy one. Until she was ten she was led to believe that Lillie was her aunt. Even when told that Lillie was her mother, the information had to be kept a secret. She was also told that her father, quite naturally, was Lillie's husband, Edward Langtry, whom they never saw and with whom they had no contact.

Perhaps the happiest times for the child were those aboard 'the Lalee', whizzing across the continent of America as part of her glamorous mother's entourage. At other times she lived with her grandmother either in Jersey or Bournemouth. In her teens Jeanne was at last allowed to call Lillie 'mother' and lived with her in London, where the two women developed a strong bond of mutual affection.

Bertie took an interest in the girl, had her presented at court and asked her to balls and parties at Buckingham Palace, both as Prince of Wales and King. Truth to tell, Jeanne was probably more socially acceptable than her notorious mother. When introduced to her, middle-aged men would often say to the lovely young woman: 'I used to know your mother', to which her reply was always the same: 'A lot of men tell me that'.

I don't think she had any illusions about her famous parent.

Through moving in the exalted circles that Bertie, now Edward VII, introduced her into, Jeanne had fallen in love. At the age of eighteen she became engaged to the thirty-three-year-old Ian Malcolm. He was a Scottish aristocrat and budding Conservative M.P. The couple's happiness was marred, however, right on the eve of their wedding.

Jeanne had been at a society party. In front of everyone there Margot Asquith had inquired what her father had given her for her birthday.

53

Thinking she meant Edward Langtry, she replied: 'But my father is dead, Lady Asquith'.

'Oh, not him,' Margot rejoined, 'Your real father, Louis Battenberg'.

Strange as it seems this, apparently, was the first inkling Jeanne had of the truth. She was used to the rumours about Bertie being her father but had always been told, quite truthfully, that they were lies. This, however, was another matter. In great distress Jeanne returned to her mother, demanding if this latest information was true and that she was, in fact, illegitimate.

Lillie was brushing her hair at the time and replied calmly: 'Well, wouldn't you rather have a man like that for a father than a drunken Irish sot?'

It killed any love her daughter had for her.

Somehow, Jeanne managed to get through the wedding where her mother, unusually, gave her away. She also settled £5,000 a year on her daughter and gave her some lavish presents. But, from then on, Jeanne wanted nothing more to do with Lillie. There were just too many lies to forgive. The parting caused both of them considerable pain.

In 1904, when she was fifty-one, Lillie, never one to forgo a challenge, set sail for a six-month tour of South Africa. She received excellent notices, reverential treatment and largely enjoyed herself. She was the first English theatre star to take a company to South Africa. As always, she was a trail blazer.

Back at home again, she was not content to rest on her laurels. Whilst her young husband Hugo and she lived increasingly more separate lives, Lillie decided to go back to America, this time not in legitimate theatre, but on the vaudeville circuit. She worked hard in little melodramas sandwiched between the dancing dogs and performing seals. Although some saw this as a come down it was highly lucrative.

Jeanne's husband, the politician and diplomat,
Sir Ian Malcolm of Poltalloch, KCMG, by Laszlo

The funeral of Edward VII in 1910

In 1907, with the death of Hugo's father (with whom the couple had eventually made up), Lillie became Lady de Bathe. The following year, she even wrote a novel entitled 'All At Sea'.

This was a frothy Edwardian piece of mistaken identity that was reviewed as 'witty, clever and bright' at the time — the review must have proved very gratifying for the new writer.

Then, in 1910, an event shook the nation. Bertie, Edward VII, died at the age of sixty-nine after a severe bout of bronchitis. Lillie watched the funeral procession pass through London from an hotel balcony. It was an impressive sight. Nine kings walked behind the gun carriage, plus someone who must have brought a lump to her throat — Louis Battenberg.

Walking directly behind the gun carriage, however, was Bertie's beloved little dog, Caesar, well-known to his master's friend, 'The Fair Lily'.

The next highlight in Lillie's eventful life came when she was sixty and starred in a silent movie in New York called 'His Neighbour's Wife'. Lillie was never frightened to try something new, but although it was quite well received, she never made another movie.

In her early sixties Lillie might have slowed down a bit — she certainly didn't need the money that her work brought in. But she was galvanised into action again with the outbreak of war in 1914.

The beginning of the war brought a momentous meeting for Lillie's daughter, Jeanne. Louis Battenberg, by then First Sea Lord, was forced to resign this position because of his German origins. Before he left London to go into exile in the country, he asked to see the daughter he had never known.

We have no record of what was said and can only guess at what father and daughter had to say to each other. Louis, of course, changed his name from Battenberg to Mountbatten, became the father of Lord Louis Mounbatten and, eventually, became the great-grandfather to our own Prince Charles. What a shame that Louis never knew, when his adopted country dismissed him out of hand, that his line would eventually produce a future King of England.

Lillie returned to the stage in a new play and, with typical generosity, donated her salary to The Red Cross.

She then crossed the Atlantic on several occasions to appear in New York and also gave various benefits for the troops in both countries, raising both money and morale in the process. Lillie was also subject to an attack by a Zeppelin raid, when on stage at the Coliseum in London. By ploughing stoically on with the performance, she quietened the panicking audience and received a standing ovation for her fortitude — another example of her physical courage.

**Le Lys, Lillie's home in Monaco**

At the end of the war, though, Lillie decided to retire from the theatre for good.

She settled for a while at Regal Lodge, her house in Kentford, but the warmer climate of the South of France was beckoning. She sold up and left England, though she would return on many occasions to see old friends.

The house she bought for her retirement years was Le Lys, a pretty Villa in Monaco. She purchased her husband a home

The Lady de Bathe

just down the road in Nice. As of old, she remained the bread winner. A sort of rapprochement took place in her final years between Jeanne and herself. The women seldom saw or spoke to each other but at least Jeanne allowed her two eldest sons to visit Lillie at Le Lys. On one of her many trips back to London she was allowed by her daughter, just once, to meet her grand-daughter, Mary Malcolm. Mary was to become one of the first BBC television continuity announcers in the early 1950s.

Whenever she was in London, looking very much a *grande dame* of the theatre, in splendid jewels and furs, Lillie would be invited to take tea with Bertie's son at Buckingham Palace. She had first known him as 'Georgie', but now he was George V. He and his wife, the formidable Queen Mary, always seemed delighted to see Bertie's sometime-lover and stalwart friend. Lillie had always promised the Royal Family that if she ever wrote her memoirs, they would be discreet. They certainly were.

'The Days I Knew' is anodyne in the extreme. In it she makes no mention that her daughter Jeanne even existed. For someone whose life was so full of sensation and scandal, her memoirs couldn't have been less so.

Separated from Hugo de Bathe, by the late 1920s Lillie was living with her butler's widow, Mrs Matilda Peat, as her friend and companion. As always, a couple of adored little dogs made up the household.

Her last years became peaceful enough, as she tended her gardens and took the occasional turn at the local casino. They were, I fear though, rather lonely. It is tempting to see her sitting surrounded by the portraits, memorabilia and photographs of the great, the good and the not so good of her younger life. Many of them had gone before her. Bertie, of course, Louis, Alix, all of her brothers — she must have wondered if she had outlived her time.

In her mid-seventies, weakened by a long illness, she contracted influenza. On February 12th, 1929, tended only by the faithful Matilda Peat, the Jersey Lily, the beauty and the scandal of her age, passed away and into the history books — a legend from Jersey both in her time and ours.

**Jeanne-Marie with her daughter, Mary**

Lillie Langtry's funeral at St, Saviour, Jersey, 1929

Lillie Langtry's signature at the height of her fame

# Afterwards

LILLIE Langtry stipulated in her will that her body should be returned to her beloved island of Jersey. She was interred with her parents and two of her brothers in the family grave in St Saviour's churchyard, close by the rectory of her birth. Her daughter, Jeanne, who had hardly spoken to her mother in the last years of her life, was her chief mourner. Lillie's husband ,Hugo, was nowhere to be seen nor sent any flowers. The funeral was a crowded affair with many local dignitaries attending. The first condolence telegram received after the news was announced was from Bertie's son and daughter-in-law — George V and Queen Mary.

In her will Lillie left many artefacts to the Jersey Museum including much of her furniture, some stage costume jewellery and the portrait of her by Edward Poynter. Jeanne received her mother's silver and there were bequests to her four grandchildren. The most substantial amount of her estate went to her companion of ten years, Matilda Peat.

Matilda Peat had a white marble bust of Lillie's youthful beauty, adorned with a Jersey lily, raised above the grave. Jeanne had a plaque placed on the church wall, dedicated in loving memory to her mother. So it seems that in death, Jeanne finally forgave her mother. For Lillie, of course, by that time, it was too late.

# Select Bibliography

Langtry, Lillie: **The Days I Knew,** 1925

Michael, Edward: **Tramps of a Scamp,** 1928

Glyn, Elinor: **Romantic Adventure,** 1936

Bland, R.H.: **Actor Soldier Poet,** 1939

Balleine, G.R.: **A Bibliographical Dictionary of Jersey,**1948

Maugham, Somerset: **A Writer's Notebook,** 1949

Dudley, E.: **The Gilded Lily,** 1959

Gerson, N.B.: **Lillie Langtry,** 1971

Porter, H.T.: **Lillie Langtry,** 1973

Brough, J.: **The Prince and the Lily,** 1975

Birkett and Richardson: **Lillie Langtry,** 1979

Morley, Sheridan: **The Great Stars ( Lillie Langtry),** 1986

Ellman, R.: **Oscar Wilde,** 1987

Aronson, T.: **The King in Love,** 1988

Hillsdon, Sonia: **The Jersey Lily,** 1993

## Recent publications by the Société Jersiaise

A Guide to the Dolmens of Jersey by Peter Hunt (paperback);
Les Écréhous, Jersey, by Warwick Rodwell (hardback); A Brief
History of Jersey, by Peter Hunt (paperback); Balleine's History
of Jersey, revised by Syvret and Stevens (hardback); Memories
of St. Ouen by C. T. Bartlett (paper booklet).

SOCIÉTÉ JERSIAISE